D1104135

Cutting Room

Also by Jessica de Koninck

Repairs

Cutting Room

by

Jessica de Koninck

Terrapin Books

Published by Terrapin Books
4 Midvale Avenue
West Caldwell, New Jersey 07006

www.terrapinbooks.com

ISBN: 978-0-9976666-0-1
LCCN: 2016946671

First edition

Cover art by Joe Waks

For my children
Isabel and Henry

Contents

The notion of directing a film is the invention of critics—the whole eloquence of cinema is achieved in the editing room.

—Orson Welles

Cutting Room

In the movie of my life
      I am played by Lauren Bacall, Vivian Leigh,
      Sigourney Weaver. Definitely
someone older, more beautiful,
      more vulnerable, more self-assured than I am.

The scene is Brandeis 1973.
The scene is Brooklyn 1958.
The scene is Montclair 1980, Trenton 2002,
my car, my yard, the bathroom, the hospital.
I can't decide.

The characters keep changing.
      My mother cut
      her wedding photos in half
      and kept the pieces without my father.

I ate a big bowl of *chili con carne* for dinner,
      then my water broke.

My hair always had its own mind,
      rejecting curl relaxer
      or a hot iron.

The moment the doctor said *cancer*
      I knew my husband was going to die.
      I woke during the night
          having started to wet the bed.

Grandma sent me to the Royal Deli
      to buy lox, *from the belly,*
      not Nova, the fat part.
      Tell them it's for Sarah. They'll know.

Paul said, *I never got my treatment.*
      The tumor had ruptured his colon.

Peritonitis set in.
He said it again and again.

On the bus ride home
after my last exam
    that first year of law school
    a man stood near the rear door
    with a brown rat on his shoulder.
    They got off at Kenmore Square.

Paul once told Kaya
    the difference between erotic and pornographic
    is the lighting.

It is the movie of the story of my life.
    How does the camera capture me
    starting to wet the bed?

At Isabel's wedding just my son and I walk her down the aisle.

The camera could focus on hands.
    I rearrange coasters on the coffee table.
They are not really coasters.
    They are tiles, from Doylestown.

That girl I suspended from a Trenton middle school.
    I can't remember her name, or what she'd done.
    Days later, her murdered body, found floating
    in a spillway behind the old factories.

Bebe kept wandering
    into the neighbor's yard
    or chasing some scent around the block
    or eating pizza crusts found on the sidewalk.
        One time she dug Henry's lost scarf out of a snowdrift.

The moment Paul died
    I knew there was no afterlife.

Eloise said, *At least he will always be*
          young and handsome.

He had beautiful hands.
          I am always falling in love
          with men's hands,
          their long fingers, rounded nails,
          curled hair at the base of the wrists.

The shot of me sitting
          alone in the living room
          gets dull fast.

I write my own screenplay
          to foretell the future.

I store the outtakes with my photo albums
          in the oak library cabinet,
          next to tax returns, death certificates,
          and deeds.

I

Translating *Klezmer*

Friday nights Grandpa talks
to God at the kitchen table,
enters the prayer book on tiptoe,
fingers the pages as if too harsh
a touch would turn them to dust,
as if words read every day were new,
as if they would leap off the paper
without his guarding gaze.

Grandpa closes his eyes, smiles
as he sings, his voice slightly nasal,
almost the sound of a clarinet.
He is certain God listens to each note.
I never thought to ask
whether God answers.

Tonight the clarinet hears
that unspoken question.
Jazz translated *klezmer* music turns
Grandpa's old faith words
into New Jersey notes,
American notes.

Chanting and moaning cries
captured across oceans,
from charred *shtetls*
on crumbled maps,
lassoed from pushcarts,

from the air shaft and the A Train
roaring underground, across the river
to me.

The clarinet whispers
my name, *Tzirelleh, Tzirelleh,*
on the lips of the candles' flames.

Tonight the clarinet says *Listen—,*
listen, God answers.

Candid

Opening the door to the old china closet
that once belonged to my grandmother, I lift
our wedding album from its shelf. Here

are my time travelers, so many now beyond time.
I had planned to write about the photograph
of Paul and his three brothers, arms around each other

and smiling. Everybody liked it. But Grandma
demands I write about her, wants me
to explain that she refused to sit

for formal portraits, refused to turn
towards the camera, refused to come
to my wedding, yet somehow there she is

at the reception. Though her nephew
took the pictures, Grandma would not
raise her eyes to him or smile. In this

solitary photo of my grandmother
she looks down at the tablecloth,
points towards something lying on a napkin.

Her rose dress, enameled beads, black framed
glasses captured when she was not looking.
Her mouth is open. She says something

I can no longer hear.

On Rosh Hashanah

Grandma, I made *kasha varnishkes*
to welcome the New Year. Wolff's *kasha*.
No, they're not in Paterson, anymore.
But when I opened the box,
there I stood in your kitchen
whisking two eggs in a ceramic bowl.
I added some salt and rendered
the chicken fat, though *schmaltz*
is not healthy. Perhaps cholesterol
clogs up memory. The odor
of buckwheat groats frying with onions
wrapped the kitchen and me
like your brown winter shawl.
I cleaned your blue dishes,
your cobalt blue glassware, good china
guarded for special occasions, like now,
while I work alone in my kitchen.

Thrill Rides

Of course I did not take the bus
to Palisades Amusement Park—
that would have meant
taking a bus to Manhattan
for a bus back to New Jersey,
and the City is more dangerous
for a thirteen-year-old girl
than standing on train tracks
with arms wide open
to see if she can jump
out of harm's way just in time
only to be struck by a train
roaring by on the opposite
track, a train traveling
at almost the speed of light, Einstein's train,
the one that explains why if I remain
in Closter, New Jersey, USA, planet Earth,
but my parents climb on board
they will become younger than me,
younger than when they told me
not to go to Palisades Amusement Park
with my friend Laurie, a fast girl,
no adult to accompany us.
Something might happen.
We might jump from the top
of the Cyclone, the world's fastest roller coaster
108 feet above the ground,
and flutter down
into the world's largest salt-water swimming pool,
two mermaids in tiny bikinis,
smiling and gasping for air,
as if we would talk to strangers,
as if anything ever happened,
because, I told you, I never went there.

Edge of the Nest

Forty-five
I watch
My teenaged daughter
Run breathless
Into our house.
Refrigerator open,
She stops,
Turns to me
Eyes wide,
It's true, she says,
My friends joke
I look just like you.
Could you get a different haircut?

Twenty-nine
I fold
Tiny white undershirts
In the second floor walkup
We rent in Belleville.
I pair
Tiny yellow booties
So everything will be ready
For this baby
For whom I will never
Be ready.
If time permits,
I will get my hair cut.

My Life as A Dog

Yes, I sleep all day.
Once in a while I get up,
walk to the kitchen,
grab some food.
Then back to bed.

Outdoors, a squirrel might catch my attention,
a rabbit, or a mole,
but after a little chase
nothing like nap time,
better yet, night time.

I dream the most amazing dreams.
Circles of dogs, snout to tail
inside circles of dogs
inside circles of dogs
dancing, or I fly.
I leap from hilltop
to hilltop. My paws
never touch the ground.

You know you have seen me dreaming.
My eyelids twitch.
My legs gyrate.
Waking life does not sustain me.
It is not enough for me to bark,
or growl or run around.

I like to cuddle
and get my belly rubbed,
but I need reverie.
I can only be myself in dreams.

How Things Work

I went to municipal court today
certain I'd see Elvis, because I read
the messages in patterns made
by missing acoustical ceiling tile
revealing an underlayer of tile,

like opposing mirrors reflecting
witnesses over and over
to the vanishing point where Elvis
must be, lost in asbestos-clad ductwork.
Elvis is the toe jam of the universe,

small but heavier than a busload
of balding Graceland tourists swinging
disposable cameras and sporting
Ground Zero ball caps. The King
is nowhere near Memphis, not

hovering over the memorial fountain
next to the kidney-shaped pool,
not swinging in the jungle room.
Set loose, he frequents workday places,
peanut butter and banana stops.

He's always the fat Elvis, never
the swivel hipped libido tickler
you might want to kiss. Most days
he passes through the neighborhood
unnoticed. He could be the lawyer

with the comb-over sitting behind me
or his client who wears sunglasses
and smells like yesterday's cigarettes.
I watch them carefully. I watch
the judge too. I don't make assumptions.

Whenever I see Elvis, I catch his eye.
Other times the law diverts
my attention. Was the driver intoxicated?
The light red? Drugs in the ashtray?
That's when I miss him.

The Man in His Undershirt Wants Me

Bruce Springsteen hangs
on the corkboard next to my desk,
right where I tacked him.
If my office had a window,
I could look outside. Instead,
we stare at each other, blindly.
The poster's his ad for Sirius radio.
Sirius, a star as far from here
as I would like to be.
Bruce's white tee says,
"Don't be so serious.
Come out and play with me."
I think, "Get serious, Boss.
In that shirt? It's wrinkled.
Why not a crisp one?
You can afford it. Someone
could iron or buy a replacement,
a black button down
like you wear on stage."
Here I sit, shut inside
listening to the drone
of the air cooling condenser.
I should take his advice,
quit my job, go to a concert,
or drive to the beach,
rip off my clothes and jump in.

Together we could break this trap.
But his legs have been airbrushed away.
Below the undershirt hem
I see only a wall
with a geometric pattern
splattered on concrete.
"You are right, Boss.

There's no place left to hide,
and you are wrong.
We're not going *to walk in the sun—*

There's nothing there, Bruce,
just paint, a picture of paint,
like the residue of an accident,
the phantom limb of an amputee."

II

Song of Jerusalem

Todah
means thanks

We cannot thank
each other enough

Yeled is boy   *yeldah* girl
yeladim children

Shalom
Hello   Goodbye   Peace

Hello peace
Goodbye peace

Goodbye children
Goodbye   goodbye

Another word I recall
after a week in *Yerushaliam*
is *shirim*

meaning songs or poems or sometimes psalms
peace poems
goodbye poems

Shirim ha Shirim
Song of Songs
Song of Solomon
Solomon the wise
Solomon the king

Most psalms are ascribed to David
Dovid Melech Yisroel
David King of Israel
a children's song

Random city signs
revise the orthography to *Dowid*

I then find it difficult
to follow directions

I cannot read road signs in Arabic
though it sounds a lot like Hebrew

Salaam   *Shalom*
Suliman   *Shlomo*   Solomon
Salaam   *Shalom*

According to the sages
the psalms are about peace
or the psalms are about war
or the psalms are about divine retribution
or faith

Shirim   Songs
        Tehillim   Psalms

I don't have many words for faith
but I named my daughter Hope

She lives here for now in Jerusalem
while I will be returning home

Hello   Hello   Hello
Goodbye   be safe
Goodbye   Goodbye

Hope is my translation for *Chashka*
one of my great-aunts murdered by the Nazis
along with her children
before I was born

Shalom   *Shalom*   *Todah*   *Shalom*
Goodbye   Peace   Goodbye   Peace   Thanks

On Exhibit

> Orphaned Art: Looted Art from the Holocaust
> in the Israel Museum

the man in Manet's portrait
gets no introduction

the painting has no title
the model no name

the man set in canvas
wears a formal dark suit

and stands trapped
in the foreground

with composition flattened
emphasizing two dimensions

except his lifelike face
angular and dark-eyed

staring off at someone
no one else can see

Jerusalem

Not the vestiges of Wall
        pressed with paper prayers
Not the Temple, the dome, the rock
Not the line for women
        the line for men

Not headscarves
Not orange groves
Not the Arab quarter
        the Jewish quarter
        the twelve stations of the Cross

Not the Cross
        nor wood
        nor nails
Not the monastery in the valley
across from the Knesset
Not *Yad Vashem*
        nor the Six Million

Not Ishmael, not Isaac
Not olive trees, not land

But a quiet booth
at a diner
in Maplewood, New Jersey
        a bowl of soup
        a buttered roll
        a cup of tea

Back Seat Driver

God creates so much noise in the back
I can't hear the radio, and he kicks
both legs to the music, rhythmically
juts his feet into my spine each fourth beat.
God, God loves the blues, the petty sorrows,
shiftless men and flashy women. Me, I'm
silent, speeding east, the seat beside me
empty. God says, it's safer in the rear,
airbags or not. I'm no fool. This banter
is one of his tests, daring me to turn
around, grab that damned foot. I face forward,
pump up the volume, choose a new station.
I know to hit the gas or slam the brake
without omniscience pushing from behind.

Flight

When I said,
That was light years ago,
as always, you corrected me.
A light year measures
distance, not time.
Why not a light mile then
or a light inch?
Something that speaks
of here to there,
not days, not years.
I don't believe in far away,
or stars,
or anything with a whimsical name
like Aldebaran or Antares or Sirius,
the dog star.
Maybe I meant dog years.
That was dog years ago,
a really long time,
as if a score or two
one way or the other means much
when we will spend almost all
eternity being dead.
The other evening
in Freehold, New Jersey,
a meteor crashed
through the roof of a suburban home,
landed on the bathroom floor
and cracked the tile. Scientists
took days to concur
yes, this is a galactic mass,
not some shard of airplane
gone haywire.
Another month passed. They changed
their minds.

They named the rock,
Freehold, New Jersey,
lacking imagination, like me.
I do not believe
cows have horns,
because I have never seen them.
And I don't believe a coin
has an even chance of landing heads
if last time it turned up tails.
I don't believe in math or science
or ruminants or Freehold, New Jersey.
I don't know why
the light goes on
when I flip the switch.
I just know that power
when it works
comes from someplace
very far away
or very long ago.

Footprints of the Stars

Maria met Jésus wandering L.A. in 1932.
The real deal, not some long-haired
messianic wannabe. He told her

he'd visited before. In '49 he panned
the Sacramento Valley, but did not stop
to watch gold rise off the ocean

the way it does in Malibu at sunset.
California reminds him of home,
warm and dry with decked-out desperados

mining Hollywood Boulevard
for cash or a needleful. One time
he was born in East L.A.

Angelinos do not weather well
away from warmth. Jésus knows
the game of life in the wilderness,

the solitude of freeways,
how to avoid snow. Hid
his face that blizzard winter

stuck outside the Donner Pass.
Now he waters arid lots.
Poinsettias with nugget hearts

bloom and bleed along the Boulevard.
Jésus watches smog rise like amnesia
over the tar pits and cultivates

fields, studded like rhinestones
among gold's rush and idols
of the silver screen. Few notice

his gardening, but in southern California
it never snows at Christmas.

Comfort Food

This noon I give thanks for fried fish
for macaroni and cheese
for dill rolls
for sweet potato pie
for this carbohydrate festival
the hair-netted ladies cooked
to get me through the afternoon
and get me home safely. I give thanks
for the cafeteria line
for steam rising off my plate
for the dishwasher smell
for the walk from my desk
across the parking lot
to the commissary
and back to my desk.
So thanks
for carrots and peas, for flakey crust
rolled by hand, for small talk
for clean trays, for breaking
a twenty, for showing up.

Jerusalem Stone

Snow buries the naked roofs of Jerusalem.

All night the wind roared like speeding trains.

City of beige and gray bleached bone white.

Bauhaus buildings lack insulation. Windows leak, furnaces weak.

Pink skin, though stone, cannot keep out the weather.

Behind proud façades, hollow cinder blocks.

Unprepared for storms, streets and shops close down.

Outdoors a few, heads bowed, press on.

Earth

Dripping, naked her child rose from the waters
Dripping, naked her child rose from the waters
Dripping, naked her child rose from the waters

Droplets, strewn from fingers, scattered everywhere
Droplets, dripped from nostrils, scattered everywhere

Her babies rolled in her mud banks
They suckled on sunshine and rainfall
She swaddled her infants in marsh grass
They slept in her caves and her meadows

And then the rain stopped falling
And then the river stopped flowing

Her children grew thin, grew tired
Their eyes turned wide and hollow
They lay in the dry weeds moaning
They held out their bony fingers
Their mouths too weak to suckle

They died with their eyes open
She raked them away like dry leaves
The sound was like footsteps or laughter
There was no water for tears

III

Labor Day

These hydrangea have turned all the colors of autumn.
Each an eye focused on the sofa, front door,
coffee table, and the window on the lake where the sky
drips melted beads into the water. The flowers
dry in an antique blue vase of hand blown glass.
My fondness now tempered, knowing before unions,
labor laws or machinery, children stoked kiln fires, sorted
colored sand. Local boys who might have gone to school
or played hooky and gone swimming, worked more cheaply
than men, took ill, died young. The cuttings and I
take refuge not far from Glassboro, Clementon, Millville,
and Clayton whose crucibles cooled decades ago.
When glory holes closed, with them went the artisans
who blew hot glass into pitchers and bowls,
bottles and doorknobs, who sheered and tweezed
frills into petals and leaves, none exactly like another,
each defect, each craze, each variation sharing
a secret of origin like the wind-stung hydrangea blossoms
crouching over the low retaining wall surrounding
Wesley Lake. Labor Day evening, all the glass
street lamp globes are reflected in the water
like little suns. Even loneliness seems a kind of joy.
Fireworks arc, ashes cascade. A light
drizzle dances on the pavement.

Reruns

Right in the living room
Jack Ruby whips out a pistol
and shoots Lee Harvey Oswald

who doubles over, falls to the floor.
Again and again the scene repeats
in black and white. Anchormen in light

shirts and dark ties pontificate
while sweating televangelists predict
damnation. James Cagney takes

a bullet too only he keeps talking.
On a different channel he sings. He dances.
Ruby stretches. Oswald collapses.

Life might be safer out in space if only
the shuttle would not explode
during breakfast, and again

after dinner and then before bed.
School Teacher, Astronaut, Indian Chief.
Starship Enterprise never blows up,

even at warp speed. Spock can
sort things out. Vulcans are part
prophet, part angel. They rely on intellect,

not feelings, and most of the time
sex is no problem. Except that
one episode with the parallel universe,

the good Spock and the bad Spock.
Hard to tell one from the other,
but God must like Spock.

Though I don't believe God
watches that much TV. Maybe
the *Twilight Zone* or the *Sopranos*.

I could stop switching
the remote and avoid those
sorry reruns; no reality shows,
no *MASH* helicopters
transport wounded GIs
across Korea. No smoke,

no screams. No towers
crumble as if in slow motion:
first one, moments later, the other.

Operating Theater

The long slender hand of the minute counter
clicks beneath five and bottoms the gravity curve.
Here the scalpel drops through blood and flesh
revealing a chewy joint to the drool shined
teeth of a fine saw blade. Closed eyes tear,
vocal chords lock, as the clock's tick
pounds its beat to morphine's slow drip.
God damn my shivering. God damn
my swollen face. This glass wall of silence
refuses to hold its breath, expanding
and contracting. Piercing shards
drain sound from the tender fluid
cradling delicate bones, the body a stone.
Strip my skin of memory, my fingertips of time.

The Dream of High Voltage in Atlantic City

Dead people ride the bus
to work each day

Tangled in electrical wire
they hang from busted windows

Foundations cracked
and no warning signs

Bones and skin and skin and bones

Reporters interview the driver whose body
drips over the bent steering wheel

Memory fails
twisted in black electrical cord

Decomposing strangled bodies
hide in shallow drainage trenches

Wet wires short circuit

Carrion and mud mingle together
shuffle of dollars and a pyrotechnic flash

Parked or broken down
near a littered asphalt alley

Daylight electrocutions
stink in the ditch

Wires knotted around bony necks
filthy hair tangled over faces

Crackle and hum and crackle and hum

Feet with no shoes
Power disconnected

No one reports them missing
They could almost be living

Magic Tricks

Despite appearances, I am not holding
a handkerchief.
It's important that I say so,
because often things are not what they seem.
It's a coat. I know you think I'm kidding.
How can a coat fit inside a handbag? No joke.
All through the winter,
this wrapping keeps me warm.
This is no riddle. I'm no Sphinx.
Even the Sphinx
was not a Sphinx, only a woman
who asked questions.
Oedipus made up his answers.
Just like a man to want
tidy explanations
for things that make no sense.
I was Eve once, you know.
I wrapped that apple in a hankie
and put it in my pocket.
Then I ate it. I did not share it.
I kept the cloth to wipe my hands.

Blast Beginning with a Line Lifted from *Howl*

Run down by the drunken taxicabs
of Absolute Reality, I stopped

minding anybody's business.
Never mind.

Repetition can be its own reward.
Sometimes silence blabs

the wrong answer. All that blankness
on the windshield, electric razor

hum of speakers, sky switched
off. No one remembers how

to answer the telephone. Its dial
floats down the river of lost metaphor

smack into the concrete wall
of Dictaphone tape. Another

static buzz wakes the monotony
of paper shuffling and the drooling

dog of false intimacy. Promise anything
in the word world. Then hit delete.

The Truth careens yellow
and checkered with worn brakes.

The Funhouse

Did you ever drive down Ocean Parkway
with the windows open on a summer
night and hear the fireworks even before
your dad parked the car and once

rode the horses at Steeplechase and twice
went down the slide but did not dare
the parachute drop? In the dreamscape
the parachute never stops falling.

The rider always travels a little
too fast. Something's off kilter about
the man with the big teeth smile.
Something that says nothing

is quite right here, a horror movie,
never feeling fully awake. It's like that
when he places the coin in her mouth and
she begins to radiate and glow

like a painted wooden saint in one
of those old off-the-beaten-track churches
where the artist didn't get the perspective
quite right, or maybe the colors, or the proportions.

You're not sure what, but the effect
is slightly askew, and that small misalignment
widens into the crack where fear enters
the room, rolls along the rotting slats

and hides with rats in broken eaves.
Remember getting lost at Coney Island.
As if in a dream, the camp bus left. You stayed.
Your brother, bless him, cried until the bus

turned around, came back and got you,
both late for his birthday party,
your mother frantic. Now the Cyclone is dead,
the Ferris Wheel dismantled. No one screams.

No reason for fear, but when the man
places the coin in your mouth,
you turn into the light. The room
begins to spin. Everything disappears.

The Golem

I understand the magic of dead things,
the resurrection of mud into matter,
desiring, as I do, to recreate you from clay,
dry grass, beach glass and sand,
wood shavings, graphite, the earth
around your plain pine box. Anything,
to bring you back. Some seed
or pod. Some breeze to breathe
life into you.

I would sit beside you. Breathless,
we would drive away. In our silence
I might forget Golem do not speak,
cannot differentiate the living
from the dead and out of ignorance
do harm. No one in this room
has risen from the dead. No one's
kiss tastes of maggots and ash,

but nothing would stop me
from blending my mortar
of grief and desire to will
you here. I am ready to die.
I would follow you anywhere.

IV

Darling,

One thing I cannot stop thinking about,
you hunched over in pain in that clawfoot
ladderback armchair you'd painstakingly
sanded, refinished, and restrung; you
chilled, doubled over, shaking, face sallow,
teeth chattering, eyes tearing, body
trembling, rocking back and forth, back and forth,
you freezing in wool cap and thick blanket.
I stand there staring, so very tired,
lightheaded as if nursing the baby,
awake in our living room, 3 a.m.
Your stomach looks larger than a pregnant
woman's. Either God's too busy to pay
attention, or pain's another good joke.

Yes, God's the star of late night comedy.
I want to shut the lights on memory,
but the video brain keeps replaying.
You're in a panic, strung out on morphine.
Hallucinations of bodies and knives
persuade you that the dead live in our house.
I do not leave. I sit and hold your hand.
You do not want more morphine or more pain.
You want photographs. You ask me to take
family photos with the new camera
that came from your brother. In the photos
your face is jaundiced. In the photos you
are dying. No one has ever seen them,
darling, except, of course, for me.

Salvage

To reverse prolapse
surgeons hold up the bladder
with the skin of a cadaver.

    Science stitches up
    what gravity pulls down.

Cadaver...

More genteel to say *organ transplant*,
better to say *donor*. Distasteful

        discussions of corneas, skin, lungs, heart.
        The cash and carry
        business that goes on at night might

get detected. But with casket closed what goes
unnoticed goes unnoticed.

        Picked clean as a car abandoned
        in Camden. Hubcaps,
        headlamps, grill work for sale.

         The business of leftovers,
         like the time we unearthed a steering arm
         and hood latch for the Renault

at a junkyard outside Worcester. Kept
that old hatchback running. So
        at the funeral home I never checked.

I did not ask to look.
With no formaldehyde, wax, or makeup,

        a night and a day would only
        make things worse. To the end

your skin remained taut,
unblemished, youthful.

Cancer and infection rot
from inside out. Your organ
donor card's a useless stub.

I did not want to look
        at you. Contaminated,
                not even good for parts.

Common Knots

He looked for the simplest ways to keep
things from falling apart: a screwdriver,
hammer and nails, wrenches,
staplers, glue gun. Taped to the file drawer,
directions for various nautical knots.
He would strip down a motor
for hours, then patiently teach
it to hum. Nothing left over
got wasted. He saved wire to make
engines run. Not his own. There's no
happy ending, just glass jars
filled with washers and screws.
Spread them out on the dining
room table. Take whatever
you think you can use.

Matisse's Paper Cut-Outs, the Swimming Pool

Our daughter phones from Brandeis. A snow day,
no school. The forecast worse than '78
when even Harvard closed its doors.
I tell her about the apartment
where we lived then, in Brighton, how we glued
blue painted paper and jute to the hallway
walls. Fish and mermaids danced,
closet and telephone waist deep in stars.

When the blizzard stopped, we grabbed
our coats, walked down three flights.
The trolley slept. Boston wrapped tight.
We walked holding hands.
Our boots sliced a path, cut out shapes
in the snow. We uncovered the car,
but with roads not plowed, nowhere to go
we cuddled back up in our little Atlantis.

Today I live elsewhere. The snow stops.
I hang up the phone. My beagle
jackknifes like a dolphin through drifts
while I begin to shovel out alone.
I quickly get thirsty, breathless from lifting.
My hands shake. I'm tired.
My head can't stop swimming.
Everything's slushy, messy, dripping.
It's just that I miss those blue fish.

The Haunted Widow

Shut up ghost! You know
how foolish I look muttering
to myself on this sidewalk.

So what if I forget things?
So what if I tell lies?
You take liberties with facts

appear out of nowhere
rely on magic.
Stop sneaking around.

I'll cover my ears with the din of traffic
and the bang of exploding
manhole covers.

I'll be deaf
to your pleas for photographs
and conversation.

So what—
So what—
So what. . .

Seal your stories up tight.
Let memory suffice.
Leave me alone.

Evolution

all morning I practiced not thinking
about you and watched a black
butterfly hover near goldenrod
watched a small brook at the turn
where water pools
before flowing downstream
little creatures cavorted
minnows   tadpoles   insects
barely visible to the eye

long ago in puddles like this
life moved from water to land
not emerging from swelling oceans
but swimming where water slowed
took a curve and began to dry up
when drought came a few survived
learned to extract oxygen from air
learned there are other ways to breathe

Tarte aux Fraises

At a sidewalk café
near the *Château Frontenac,*
I slip a forkful of quiche
on my tongue, sip
a *vin rosé.* The couple
at the next table holds
onto their last syllables.
Another summer of strawberries,
the drive from *Montréal* to *Québec,*
empty except *Trois Rivières*
and its factory smells.
Tired and hungry, we stopped
once for lunch at a roadside place,
a dark bar with a jukebox
and weathered truckers.
Our honeymoon. We were
so young. You were alive.
The waitress brought us
jambon beurre
on fresh baked bread
with hand-churned butter
and home-cured ham,
then *tarte aux fraises,*
the berries picked that morning.
She sent us away smiling.
Au revoir. Au revoir.

For years when driving
to *Québec,* we ventured off
the main road, but somehow never
found that place again.
No name or sign or landmark
came to mind. The tablecloths
were plastic, checkered,
red and white. The light

coming from the kitchen
seemed very bright. When
we got there, it was late.
A truck stop, in *Trois Rivières,*
could have been anywhere.

Now, after eight years, I take
that drive alone.
All along the shoulder, signs
for strawberries, pick your own.

V

The Thing with Elvis

This isn't really about Elvis.
Elvis is dead, demised, defunct,
as deceased as any of us can be,
buried and decomposed,
turning dirtward.

I got tired of Elvis
after *Hound Dog*,
when he came back
from the army and his music
slowed down. By the time
sex caught up with me, Elvis
was zipped into spandex so tight
his wrists and ankles swelled.

So now it's Bruce––
tonight at Giant's
Stadium, me, Bruce
and fifty thousand friends,
mouthing words
we know by heart.
My kids would blush.

Isn't that the *runaway American dream*,
to listen to a great garage band,
make out, get a little high
without thinking too hard,
without getting soft like Elvis?

Max Weinberg smashes his drums.
I like that. I like sidekicks;
backup players who keep the groove going
without spotlight or giant screen.
Easy in this crowd to forget

they're really there.
I watch him scan the band.

Yes, Bruce has still got it,
and says so, grinning
for the camera, egging us to beg
for one more encore while Max

crashes cymbals, stomps pedals,
kind of looks like someone I might
have dated in college, or what that guy
would look like 35 years later
if he still looked pretty good.
Almost everyone here
seems my age or older.

The thing with Elvis,
the man could dance. His hips were magic.
Bruce just keeps rocking,
never goes acoustic. Never *Nebraska*.

The crowd pulses, not like Elvis.
Max is alive. Bruce is alive.
But I don't get to meet them.
They stay on stage. I take them on faith.
I rely on binoculars. My seat's Level 3,
Row L. They could be ghosts
like Elvis, flickering match lights
of my imagination, though no one,
I think, has left the building.

Another New Year

I invite you to dinner for Rosh Hashanah

> I will bake apple cake
> I will make *tzimmes*
> I will make pot roast

Clover, tupelo, orange blossom

> I will infuse each dish with honey
> Honey for sweetness
> Honey for hope

Sage, eucalyptus, sourwood

I will invite

> My mother. My father is dead
> My children
>> who may have to work
>> and not come for dinner
> My sister, her husband, her children

Acacia, alfalfa, pumpkin blossom

They will treat you like family

> They will try not to ask
> too many questions

> We will dip
> crisp apple slices in honey

Camelthorn, clover, lavender

I will not say
            being happy makes me sad
I will not say
            anything about love

        Fireweed, linden, wildflower

Traffic Jam

Summer sits southbound, stuck in shore traffic
back to back, bumper to bumper,
all the same from here to Long
Beach Island. Radiators overheating,
lopsided piles of bicycles and boogie boards
towels, umbrellas, and water wings.
I put mine on to fly
above the crowd, take me
where I want to be,
secluded on a beach.
Daydreams melt like ice
cream cones one after another,
faster than I lick around the edges,
and you, Dreamsicle, nowhere
to be seen, except in my imagination
and memory. The boardwalk
at night, walking you
out of my mind.
Stuck here on the highway
as temperature rises
makes me think more
not less. My orange wings
bounce on the water. Waves
roll and break into white soft serve
less gritty than chocolate,
more the way I think of you.
A touch salty with an aftertaste
that stays with me on this road
even when I think I passed
my exit. You are sea foam.
I am a flying fish.

The Delaware at Morrisville

The welders wove steel
    wires across the river.
        Cars thread from shore to shore.

I stroll midway
between clouds and water,
beaming as if I'd gotten a raise, as if
I were in love.

What else is there to say?
That the bridge is painted green
to look like copper, like the Statue of Liberty
with its patina of rust

oxidizing in the afternoon sun.
She does a slow burn
motionless to the unaided eye,
and even a stop action camera,
or a series of Muybridge photos
slowed down a thousandfold
would not be slow enough
to capture the disintegration
of that metal arm now raised
high above the river.
My whole life
will take less time than that.

For now I am content;
the bridge looks like lace,
the sky piercing blue.
Water glints its sequined tears.

        Just this sunny day,
    a walk across the bridge
and back again.

If He Proposes Say *Yes*

Consider the sparrows
picking at insects.
Their small high-pitched chirps
dot the landscape with worry.

Consider the sparrows
hidden in hedges,
tiny dull warblers
of suburban afternoons.

Watch them swallow seeds,
sip from shallow puddles.
How easily they scare
when a sleek cat wanders by,

climbs into a tree,
searches for dinner,
stretches out a paw
agitating the branches.

Consider the sparrows
perched on phone wires.
Even through winter
they nest in front yards.

Crocuses

Sorry, this is not the first time snow fell almost
each March day. Sorry, a few broken shingles, a few
loose gutters, mean a worse year than some.
It may take years to rebuild the boardwalk, beachfront,
fish pier, and the low retaining wall around the lake.
Splintered beams and broken concrete benches
are stacked like prosthetic legs. But the crocuses
do not care. They have been hiding underground.
Alabaster, gold, and lilac camouflaged by dirt. Today
they sunbathe as you wrap your scarf more tightly,
pull up your coat collar. Look, the swan boats, freshly
painted, have returned to Wesley Lake. Winter-weary
lovers paddle across and back. A little chill excites.
Across each front yard violet confetti, *Look at me*,
crocuses shout, among bare branches and gray grasses.
Look at me! I'm back.

Repairs

I almost went to visit the cemetery,
but you are not really there,
just what might be left
of the parts. When you died,
your brother refused to look
at the body. *That's not Paul,
anymore,* he said.
                      I did look.
I sat and examined you closely,
a moment after you died, an hour
after, several hours after.
You would have done the same
for me, taking note of the details
of the flesh after life, what changed,
what remained the same.
Your hair still smelled like your hair
when the men came to remove
the body. They would not let me
watch you go.

Instead of the cemetery I went
to Home Depot since it's on the same street,
but not as far away. How funny
you would find me, navigating hardware,
electrical, plumbing supplies.
The whole place smells like men.
I miss that.
                   I walked past the yard bags
three times before I found them
and did not know to buy a switch
along with the light. How you loved
meandering the overstocked
aisles, inspecting the intricacies
of toggle bolts, checking lumber for knots

and warping. It's my turn now.
I am becoming accomplished
in the small details of living alone.
I have learned to shim a table,
tighten a faucet, drill a hole.

Going Around in Circles

I ride the Ferris wheel, because I am afraid
of heights, of climbing up and falling down
and stopping in mid-sentence.

The line is long. The ride is short,
yet somehow I've persuaded my friend
to join this circular assault

upon the top of Ocean City. Most riders
are children, but we are older women
whose cataracts shape haloes around

the blinking lights visible for miles
from this island. With each dizzying
rotation these handmade stars

look more beautiful to me. There
are so many things I am not supposed
to do like hurtling into the edge

of motion sickness, so I ride the Ferris
wheel remembering there are two ways to die
inside this flying car: electricity

and gravity, although I know every morning
when the giant wheel has stopped,
spider-workers climb thin inner girders

to check welds, bolts, and sealants
that support the crumbly frame. Rust's
a kind of burning, cool to the touch,

turns iron into dust. From up here
I can almost make out Philadelphia
where my daughter lives, but if I relax

my grip to wave, no one below
will see me. My chair will start
to sway. Instead of looking down,

I watch the ocean until it stops
at the curve at the world's edge, and then
I spin. These relics of the Gilded Age

fascinate me: skyscrapers, steel
skeletons, amusement parks.
I'm a bicycle aerialist on a climbing

wheel. Steel spokes tense
and compress, twenty stories
above the boardwalk. Then the car

drops and rises, drops, circling
three times before stopping,
unloading, loading until

each seat fills. It's a carousel
upended with calliope of wind.
I think about acceleration. My mind

goes in circles. In descent velocity
increases at constant speed.
I understand some physics, but I find it

hard to breathe. I ride the Ferris wheel,
and thrill builds a memory.
I ride the wheel, and I hold on.

Acknowledgments

Grateful acknowledgment goes to the following publications in which these poems first appeared:

Adanna: "Another New Year," "Common Knots," "Salvage," "Song of Jerusalem," *"Tarte aux Fraises"*
The Apple Valley Review: "Comfort Food"
Arc: "Jerusalem Stone"
Compass Rose: "Darling"
Edison Literary Review: "My Life as a Dog," "Translating *Klezmer*"
Exit 13: "The Delaware at Morrisville," "Thrill Rides"
Jewish Currents: "Evolution," "Jerusalem"
The Ledge: "Flight"
Lips: "On Exhibit"
Literary Mama: "Edge of the Nest"
Mad Poets Review: "Bullion"
Paterson Literary Review: "The Man in His Undershirt Wants Me," "On Rosh Hashanah"
Poetica Magazine: "Back Seat Driver"
Poetry Magazine: "Traffic Jam"
Pop Fic Review: "Reruns"
The Stillwater Review: "Matisse's Paper Cut-Outs, the Swimming Pool"
U.S. 1 Worksheets: "Earth," "Magic Tricks," "Operating Theater"
Valparaiso Literary Review: "The Funhouse"

"Blast Beginning with a Line Lifted from *Howl*" appeared in *The Final Lilt of Songs: A Poetry Anthology* (South Mountain-Watchung Poets, 2008).

"Edge of the Nest" appeared in *Coming of Age: A Treasury of Poems, Quotations and Readings on Growing Up* (Skinner House, 2007) and in *Regrets Only: Contemporary Poets on the Theme of Regret* (Little Pear Press, 2006).

"Footprints of the Stars" appeared in *The Breath of Parted Lips: Voices from the Frost Place,* Vol. II (CavanKerry Press, 2004).

"The Golem" appeared in *The Doll Collection* (Terrapin Books, 2016).

"Labor Day" appeared in *Union: Poems by Forty Finalists from the 2014 Alexander and Doris Raynes Poetry Competition* (Blue Thread, 2014).

"Repairs" and "Salvage" appeared in *The Widows' Handbook* (Kent State University Press, 2014).

"The Golem" and "Repairs" appear in *Repairs*, a limited edition chapbook, Finishing Line Press.

About the Author

Cutting Room is Jessica de Koninck's first full-length collection. She is also the author of a chapbook, *Repairs,* from Finishing Line Press. Her poems have been finalists in the *Dobler, Raynes,* and *Ledge* poetry contests. Earlier collections have been finalists or semi-finalists in the *Black Lawrence, Juniper Creek,* and *Press 53* book contests. A former attorney, she has served as counsel to the Trenton and South Orange/Maplewood public school districts in New Jersey. She is also the former government relations director for the New Jersey Department of Education. She served on both the Montclair town council and the Library Board. Currently the president of the Montclair, New Jersey, Board of Education, she teaches School Law and Policy at Kean University. She holds an MFA from Stonecoast, University of Southern Maine.

www.jessicadekoninck.com

CPSIA information can be obtained at www.ICGtesting.com
Printed in the USA
LVOW11s1134280816

502186LV00003B/452/P